Hi! I'm Dora and this is my friend Boots. We'[re at the] carnival. We need to collect 10 tickets to go on the Rainbow Slide. Will you help us? Great! We'll need the special decoder inside this book. We can use it to see the hidden answers that the arrow is pointing to.

Don't forget to watch for Swiper the fox. If you see him, say, "Swiper, no swiping!"

I got one ticket when I entered the carnival and so did Boots. Help us count how many we have together. Write the number then use the decoder to see if you're right.

1 + 1 = ___

Smart adding! To win more tickets, we can play the games at the carnival.

Boots won two tickets by throwing two beanbags in the clown's mouth. Let's add two more tickets to our total.

2 + 2 =

I got four beanbags in the clown's mouth. So that's another four tickets!

+ 4 =

Isa gave Boots one of her tickets. Let's add it to our eight tickets. How many tickets do we have all together?

$$8 + 1 = \text{\underline{\hspace{2cm}}}$$

Adding is great. It's just like counting!
Add these numbers then draw a line to
the ticket that shows the total.

$2 + 1 =$ __3__

$3 + 2 =$ ___

$3 + 3 =$ ___

$5 + 2 =$ ___

$9 + 1 =$ ___

6

3

10

5

7

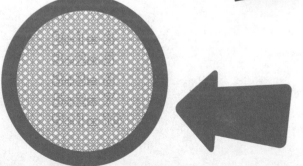

We paid four tickets to ride the Ferris Wheel.
How many are left?

Mark an **X** on the number of tickets we used then count the number that is left. Write the number and use the decoder to check the answer.

$$9 - 4 = \underline{}$$

I used one ticket to buy cotton candy. Mark an **X** on one ticket then write how many are left.

$$5 - 1 = \underline{}$$

Subtracting is like counting backwards! Subtract these numbers then draw a line to the ticket that shows the total.

4 - 2 =   2

4 - 1 =

7 - 1 =

9 - 2 =

10 - 2 =

3

7

2

8

6

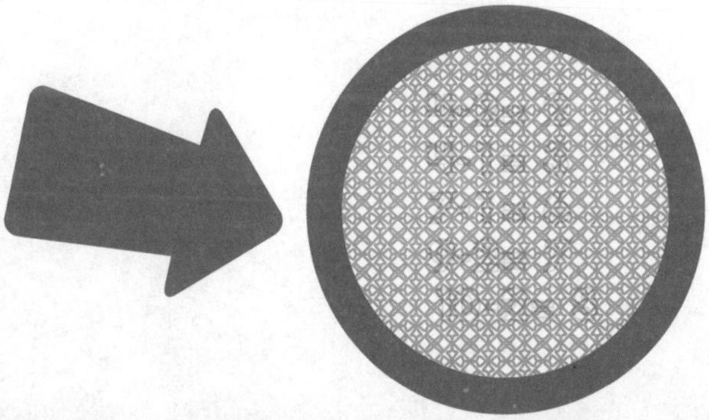

I knocked down two milk bottles and Boots knocked down three. How many did we knock down together? Color the milk bottles and write the number.

We won a ticket for every milk bottle that we knocked down. That's five more tickets! Add them to the four we have left from before.

$$\begin{array}{r} 4 \\ +\,5 \\ \hline \end{array}$$

Wow, adding down is the same as adding across! Add these numbers and circle the correct answer below each problem.

$$\begin{array}{r} 2 \\ +2 \\ \hline \end{array}$$

④ 5 6

$$\begin{array}{r} 6 \\ +2 \\ \hline \end{array}$$

7 8 9

$$\begin{array}{r} 5 \\ +4 \\ \hline \end{array}$$

5 7 9

$$\begin{array}{r} 1 \\ +1 \\ \hline \end{array}$$

1 2 3

$$\begin{array}{r} 5 \\ +1 \\ \hline \end{array}$$

6 8 10

$$\begin{array}{r} 4 \\ +6 \\ \hline \end{array}$$

8 9 10

Look, we're riding on the Merry-Go-Round! It cost us two tickets. Cross out the two tickets we spent. Now how many tickets do we have left?

$$\begin{array}{r} 9 \\ -\ 2 \\ \hline \end{array}$$

The ice cream stand had eight cones and we bought two.
How many more ice cream cones can the stand sell?
Cross out two and write how many are left.

8
-2
___

Uh oh, I see Swiper. That sneaky fox will try to swipe our ice cream! Say, "Swiper, no swiping!"

Thanks for helping us stop Swiper!

We had seven tickets, but we spent four on ice cream. Help us figure out how many tickets we have left and write the number. Then use the decoder to check the answer.

Subtracting down is the same as subtracting across! Subtract these numbers and circle the correct answer for each problem.

9
- 2
———
5 6 (7)

5
- 4
———
1 2 3

7
- 1
———
6 7 8

10
- 2
———
7 8 9

4
- 2
———
1 2 3

10
- 1
———
7 8 9

We need 10 tickets to go on the Rainbow Slide but we only have three. If we subtract three from ten we can figure out how many more tickets we need. Circle the three tickets that we have and count the rest to see how many more we need.

I hit the bull's-eye and won the jackpot! Color and count the tickets on the sign. Then write the number and add the three we had from before.

+3

JACKPOT

Hooray! We did it! We collected 10 tickets. Now we can go on the Rainbow Slide! Solve each problem and use the code to color the slide.

$2 + 3 =$

$8 - 4 =$

$7 - 1 =$

$2 + 1 =$

Make sure you check the answers before coloring the slide.

We had such a great time at the carnival. Thanks for helping us!

Contents

Seek and Find

Can you find these objects in your book?

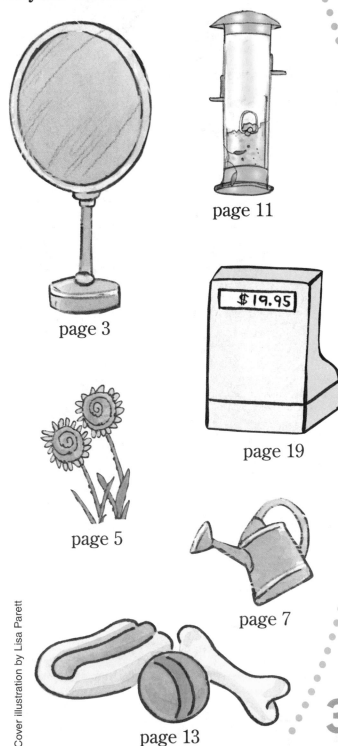

page 3

page 11

$19.95

page 19

page 5

page 7

page 13

Cover illustration by Lisa Parett

Solving Hidden Pictures puzzles develops figure-ground perception and improves the ability to establish object constancy and size relationships. Educators have shown that working on these puzzles can enhance a child's attention to detail, reinforce good work habits, increase word knowledge, and aid in developing self-confidence.

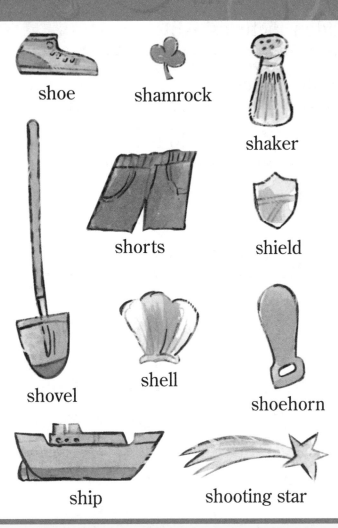

shoe

shamrock

shaker

shorts

shield

shovel

shell

shoehorn

ship

shooting star

Illustrated by John Nez

Try to write some of your favorite words that begin with sh on the lines below.

sh _____

sh _____

sh _____

sh _____

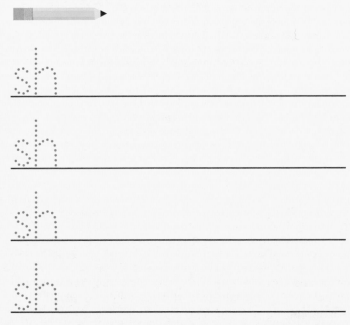

Can you find the 10 objects hidden in the picture that begin with the letters sh? Sharp! Answers on page 30

3

These 8 funny things are happening in the scene.
Can you find them all? Answers on page 30

Imagine and Draw

What is the silliest instrument someone might play? Draw a picture of it here.

CRAYON

Illustrated by Viki Woodworth

6 Stacy's Tree House

Stacy and her friends like to play in her tree house after school.

Can you find these hidden objects on the next page?

Answers on page 30

glove

dustpan

ruler

frog

teacup

baseball bat

cupcake

fish

Scavenger Hunt

Here are some more things to find:

 A football

Three butterflies

 Two birds

A whisk broom

Four red flowers

 Two pockets

 A strainer

A bowl

Can you find the Hidden Pictures below? When you finish, you can color in the

rest of the scene. ‖ CRAYON ‖ Answers on page 30

Illustrated by Larry Daste

Color in a mouse in this box each time you find a mouse in the picture.

Connect the dots from Ⓐ to Ⓩ. When you are done, help the mouse find his way from START to FINISH.

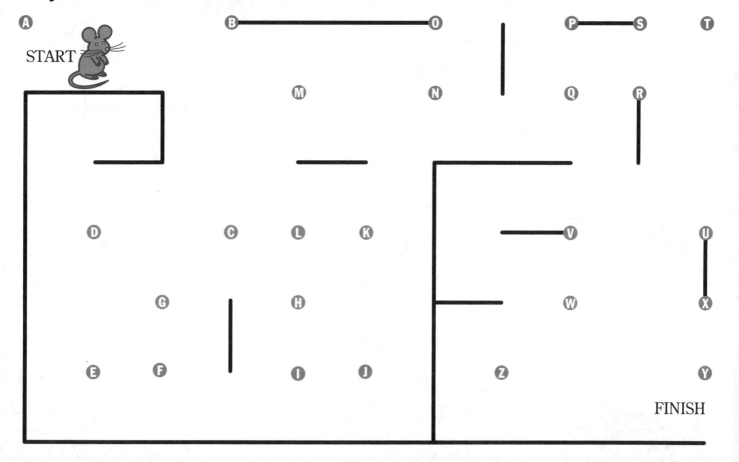

Illustrated by Mary Sullivan

Kylie and Jay are learning to take good care
of their new puppy, Pete.

Can you find 8 Hidden Pictures® on the next page? Answers on page 31

saucepan

eyeglasses

feather

artist's
brush

lollipop

cupcake

stamp

peanut

**Use your crayons to draw the dog who lives
in this doghouse.** ‖ CRAYON ‖

Write the name of the dog here._____

**Hidden Pictures time to rhyme.
You can find them every time.**

A furry  **squirrel** is hiding here.

A **skateboard** you can ride is near.

Now find the little sandy  **crab**

and a **dog leash** you can grab.

Try to spot a fuzzy **peach**

and an **umbrella** for the beach.

Look and find a  **sugar bowl**

and a fine old **fishing pole**.

You're almost done, just spy a **lock**

and a baby's teeny  **sock**.

**You first found one and then the rest.
Hip! Hip! Hooray! You are the best!**

Answers on page 31

Illustrated by Judith Moffatt and Bill Hoffman

Can you find the Hidden Pictures below? When you finish, you can color in the

rest of the scene. CRAYON Answers on page 31

Illustrated by Ellen Appleby

Sam has outgrown his shoes. Today he and his mom are shopping for a new pair.

Can you find these items in the picture on the next page? Be sure to find the right number of each.

Answers on page 31

1 bench

2 black shoes

3 brown sandals

4 boots

5 yellow boxes

6 sneakers

Color in each shape that has a red dot with a red crayon. CRAYON
Color in each shape that has a yellow dot with a yellow crayon. CRAYON
When you are done, you will see something Sam's mother has promised to buy him when they finish shopping.

Illustrated by Monica Wellington

$19.95

$ 20 $

A
Hidden Pictures®
Rebus Story by
Clare Mishica

Terrence went to the carnival with his mom and his sister, Monique. First, Monique rode the roller coaster. It zipped around the curves like a shiny green **snake**.

"I'll watch," said Terrence. "The roller coaster makes my stomach feel like I swallowed a **butterfly**."

Next, Monique rode the Ferris wheel.

"I'll watch," said Terrence. "I do not want to go up high in the sky like a **bird**."

Then Monique rode the Tilt-a-Whirl. Her red car spun around like a toy **top**.

"I'll watch," said Terrence. "The Tilt-a-Whirl makes my head feel dizzy."

Finally, Mom said, "I know which ride you will like. Come with me."

They walked past the 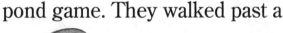 **fish** pond game. They walked past a **balloon** seller. They walked past the **hot dog** stand. Just beyond the **lemonade** stand, they saw a man wearing a cowboy hat. He had five spotted ponies with saddles on their backs.

"How about this kind of ride?" asked Mom.

"Yes!" laughed Terrence. "A pony ride is the perfect ride for me!"

Illustrated by Marsha Winborn

guitar

heart

hammer

star

hot dog

butterfly

Illustrated by Maja Andersen

Each object is hidden two times—once in each scene. We found and circled the butterflies. Can you find the others? Answers on page 32

23

candy cane   umbrella   crown   flower   fan   doughnut

Can you find the Hidden Pictures below? When you finish, you can color in the

Tall Ships

rest of the scene. **CRAYON** Answers on page 32

Illustrated by Timothy Davis

Camille takes her camera wherever she goes.
Today she is taking pictures at the aquarium.

Can you find these shapes in the picture on the next page? Answers on page 32

What is your favorite sea animal? Draw a picture of it here. CRAYON
Be sure to write your name on your drawing when you are finished.

Sea Friends

Hidden Pictures®

These horseshoe players are hoping to make a ringer.

There are 12 objects hidden in this picture. How many can you find?

Answers on page 32

mushroom

cheese

heart

cherry

golf ball

comb

crown

paintbrush

key

crayon

glove

pencil

The names of the 12 objects are hidden below. Some are across. Others are up and down. Find and circle each word.

d	z	p	c	o	m	b	g
c	r	a	y	o	n	j	o
h	c	i	k	p	q	h	l
e	h	n	e	e	c	e	f
r	e	t	y	n	r	a	b
r	e	b	x	c	o	r	a
y	s	r	d	i	w	t	l
z	e	u	q	l	n	d	l
m	u	s	h	r	o	o	m
q	z	h	g	l	o	v	e

Cover

Hidden Pictures® ABC pages 2–3

Silly Concert page 5

Stacy's Tree House pages 6–7

Scavenger Hunt

A football
Look near the dog.

Three butterflies
One is near the dog.
One is near the boy in the striped shirt.
One is near the girl wearing a cape.

Two birds
One is in the tree.
One is on a fence post.

A whisk broom
Look on the tree house.

Four red flowers
Two are in front of the tree.
One is near a boy.
One is near the football.

Two pockets
Look on the girl wearing overalls.

A strainer
It is on somebody's head.

A bowl
A boy is holding it.

Ice Skaters pages 8–9

Mouse Search pages 10–11

It's a maze!

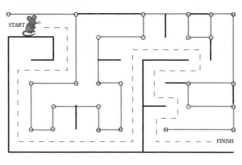

New Puppy page 13

Hidden Pictures® Rhymes pages 14–15

It's an ice-cream cone!

Square Dance pages 16–17

Shoes for Sam page 19

A Ride for Terrence page 21

Double Hidden Pictures® pages 22–23

Tall Ships pages 24–25

Find the Shapes page 27

Hidden Pictures Hidden Words pages 28–29

Contents

Seek and Find

Can you find these objects in your book?

page 27

page 15

page 8

page 21

Cover illustration by Ellen Appleby

SOAP

page 19

page 11

Solving Hidden Pictures puzzles develops figure-ground perception and improves the ability to establish object constancy and size relationships. Educators have shown that working on these puzzles can enhance a child's attention to detail, reinforce good work habits, increase word knowledge, and aid in developing self-confidence.

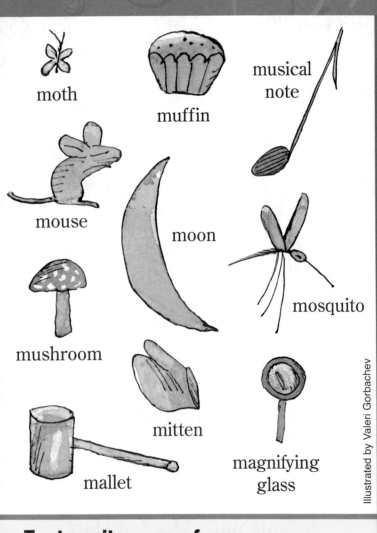

moth

muffin

musical note

mouse

moon

mushroom

mosquito

mitten

mallet

magnifying glass

Illustrated by Valeri Gorbachev

Try to write some of your favorite words that begin with m on the lines below.

m _____

m _____

m _____

m _____

These 8 funny things are happening in the scene.
Can you find them all? Answers on page 30

Imagine and Draw

What is the silliest thing you might see in a school?
Draw a picture of it on this book cover.

CRAYON

Illustrated by Nathan Y. Jarvis

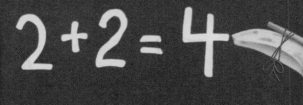

Ryan and Alexis are finding all kinds of surprises in the attic.

Can you find these hidden objects on the next page? Answers on page 30

bat

puppet

slice of pizza

key

lollipop

banana

duck

pickle

Scavenger Hunt
Here are some more things to find:

A flashlight

A string of beads

An umbrella

Six pink flowers

An alarm clock

Four hats

A lock without a key

Two green books

Can you find the Hidden Pictures below? When you finish, you can color in the

rest of the scene. **CRAYON** Answers on page 30 Illustrated by R. Michael Palan

Color in a crayon in this box each time you find a crayon in the picture.

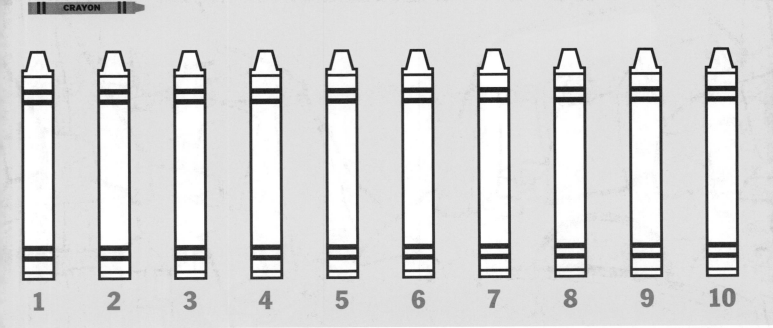

CRAYON

1 2 3 4 5 6 7 8 9 10

Connect the dots from ❶ to ㉚ to make something that you might draw with a crayon.

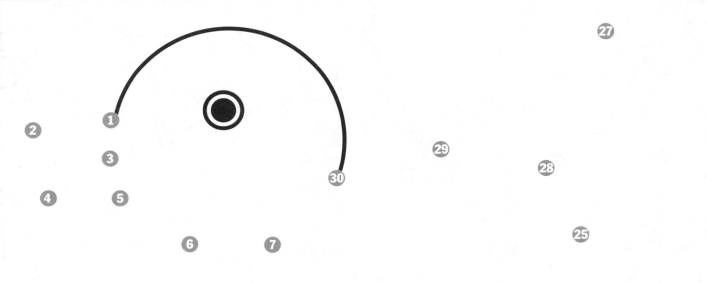

David has a job walking dogs in his neighborhood.
Today his sister Madeline is helping him.

Can you find 8 Hidden Pictures® on the next page?

Answers on page 31

screw

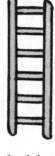

ladder

toothbrush

carrot

fork

hot dog

shoe

heart

Illustrated by Ron Lieser

What kind of dog is on the end of the leash?
Draw a picture of it here. ▏▏ CRAYON ▏▏ ►

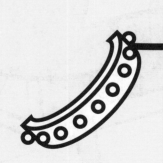

Hidden Pictures time to rhyme.
You can find them every time.

Can you see a number two?

Now look until you find this shoe.

Try to spy a candy cane.

Seek and find a paper plane.

To row a boat you'll need that oar.

You use a broom to sweep the floor.

Do you see a talking parrot

And a crunchy orange carrot?

To finish, find a cooking whisk

And a small computer disk.

You first found one and then the rest.
Hip! Hip! Hooray! You are the best!

Answers on page 31

Illustrated by Lisa Parett

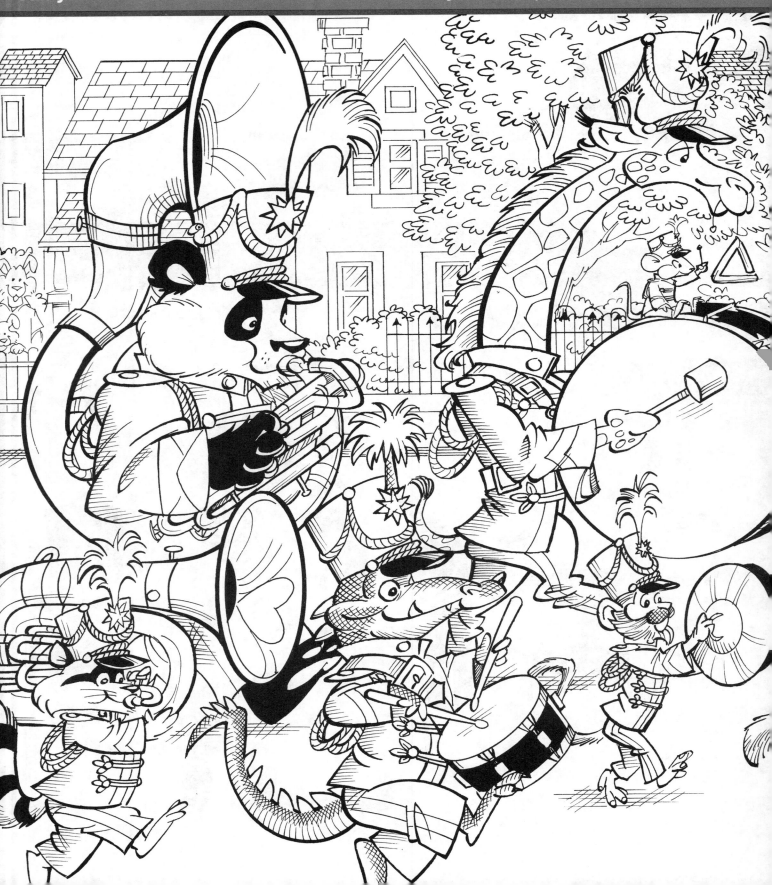

rest of the scene. **CRAYON** Answers on page 31 Illustrated by Rocky Fuller

Joshua is helping his mother wash and put away everyone's socks.

Can you find these items in the picture on the next page? Be sure to find the right number of each. Answers on page 31

1 white sock   **2** red socks   **3** blue socks

4 checkered socks   **5** striped socks   **6** polka-dot socks

Illustrated by Monica Wellington

Color in each shape that has a red dot with a red crayon. ▮▮ CRAYON ▮▮
Color in each shape that has a black dot with a black crayon. ▮▮▮ CRAYON ▬
When you finish, you will see something else Joshua helps to wash.

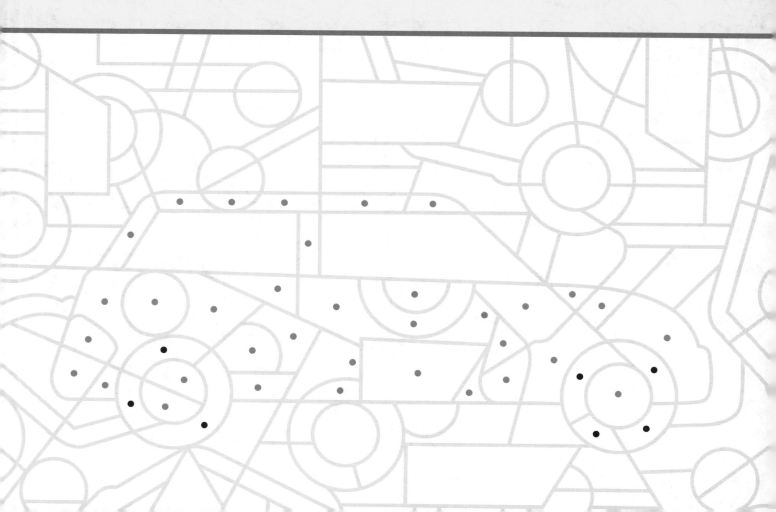

Rabbit buttoned her sweater. "My friend Squirrel will be here soon. We are going for a walk," she said. "Now where is my hat?"

Rabbit opened her **hatbox** and looked inside. There was tissue paper in her hatbox. But no hat.

Rabbit looked under the bed. She found a  **slipper** and a **book** under the bed. But no hat.

Rabbit looked on the hook by the door. There was a **scarf** on the hook by the door. But no hat. "Where could my hat be?" asked Rabbit.

Rabbit looked under the chair. She found a  **pencil** and a  **hairbrush** under the chair. But no hat.

Rabbit looked in the kitchen closet. There was a **broom** in the closet. But no hat.

The **doorbell** rang.

"Good morning," said Squirrel. "Are you ready to go for a walk?"

"I am not ready. I have looked everywhere. But I cannot find my hat," said Rabbit.

A Hidden Pictures® Rebus Story by Jeffie Ross Gordon

"I know where you did not look," said Squirrel.

"Where?" asked Rabbit.

"In the mirror," said Squirrel.

Rabbit ran to the mirror. "Of course," she said. "How silly! My hat is where it belongs. My hat is on my head."

Then Rabbit and Squirrel went for a walk.

Illustrated by Maggie Swanson

Can you find the hidden objects from the story in this scene? Answers on page 32

traffic
light

butterfly

jewel

hubcap

pear

tadpole

Illustrated by Linda Davick

Each object is hidden two times—once in each scene. We found and circled the pears. Can you find the others? Answers on page 32

suitcase

grapefruit

can

frying
pan

car

spoon

Can you find the Hidden Pictures below? When you finish, you can color in the

Skis and Snowboards

rest of the scene. CRAYON Answers on page 32

Illustrated by Timothy Davis

Camille takes pictures wherever she goes.
Today she is at a costume party.

Can you find these shapes in the picture on the next page? Answers on page 32

What costume would you like to wear? Draw a picture of it here.

CRAYON

Be sure to write your name on your drawing when you are finished.

Hidden Pictures®

At the amusement park, Nick and Taylor love riding the merry-go-round. What is your favorite ride?

There are 12 objects hidden in this picture. How many can you find?
Answers on page 32

envelope

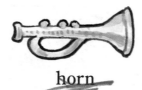
horn

cap

The names of the 12 objects
are hidden below. Some are across.
Others are up and down.
Find and circle each word.

flag

ice cream

bell

mitten

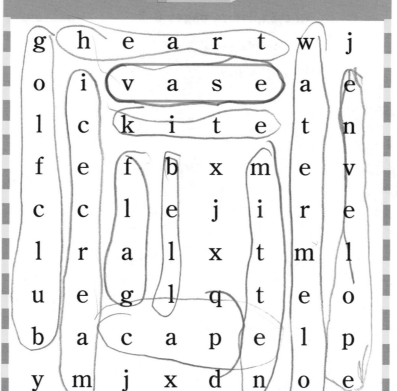

```
g   h   e   a   r   t       w       j
o   i   v   a   s   e       a       e
l   c   k   i   t   e       t       n
f   c   f   b   x   m       e       v
c   e   l   e   j   i       r       e
l   r   a   l   x   t       m       l
u   e   g   l   q   t       e       o
b   a   c   a   p   e       l       p
y   m   j   x   d   n       o       e
j   q   z   h   o   r   n       q
```

golf club

vase

watermelon

heart

kite

Illustrated by Ellen Appleby

Cover

Hidden Pictures® ABC pages 2–3

Silly School page 5

Attic Explorers pages 6–7

Scavenger Hunt

A flashlight
Look behind the boy.

A string of beads
The girl is wearing them.

An umbrella
It is on the floor.

Six pink flowers
Look on a hat.

An alarm clock
It is on top of a bundle of papers.

Four hats
The boy and the girl are wearing one each.
Two more are near the cat.

A lock without a key
Look on the green trunk.

Two green books
They are near the umbrella.

Canyon Riders pages 8–9

Crayon Search pages 10–11

It's a bird!

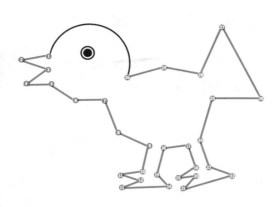

Dog-Walking page 13

Hidden Pictures® Rhymes pages 14–15

Lots of Socks page 19

It's a car!

Marching Band pages 16–17

Answers

Rabbit's Missing Hat page 21

Double Hidden Pictures® pages 22–23

Skis and Snowboards pages 24–25

Find the Shapes page 27

Hidden Pictures Hidden Words pages 28–29